MASS

AWAKENING

What's Really Going On?
2020 - 30 Minute Synopsis

John McIntosh

Published by ONE-SELF Productions

ISBN: 9798554979019

We gratefully acknowledge **Solveig Larsen** for
providing the cover image

INDEX

PREFACE - 4

CHAPTER ONE – THE CURRENT MASS
AWAKENING - 9

CHAPTER TWO – THE SECOND
AWAKENING - 31

CHAPTER THREE - THE 'REAL'
AWAKENING - 38

ABOUT THE AUTHOR - 49

LINKS - 50

TESTIMONIALS - 51

PREFACE

HUMANITY IS RAPIDLY AWAKENING FROM A DEEP SLEEP

In night-time dreams you are *usually* not aware that you are dreaming, but occasionally you *may **become aware*** that you *are* dreaming. This is known as a **lucid dream**. This is what is now occurring throughout humanity in the *dream* most call *reality* ... **the waking dream**.

This dream is ancient in terms of clock time and through a multitude of dream-lifetimes the **Real YOU** has returned again and again to *play in this field of dreams* in order to *know* **IT SELF**. This knowing is not about a *personal self* ... it is about the **ONE Reality** *in which* the **universal/world dream** is occurring.

This **ONE** is also known as *Consciousness, God, SELF, I AM, Love* and many other names.

YOU are this ONE

There *is* nothing **but** this ONE and it is *Pure Emptiness* while having *infinite potential*. In order to know **IT SELF, IT** requires a *frame of reference* with which to experience this potential. Since IT is empty or nothing, this frame of reference is an **illusion**, a **holographic projection** on what may be considered the *screen of consciousness.*

All this is within the ONE YOU Are

ONE or YOU manifested this illusion by having an idea called **separation**. This provided the possibility of a *from here to there* phenomena, which in turn manifested another illusion called **time and space**, *since* *it takes time* and space to traverse one separated thing or experience to another.

ONE/YOU then entered the **entire illusion** giving it a *transient life* [things that come and go] and then - *forgot* IT SELF for a season so that IT could *fully experience* every possibility **as if** it were real. This has been called *"The fall of man"* but was simply the *"Fall of Conscious Awareness"* **of** IT SELF. This *illusory* separation produced the **contrast** required for the **SELF to know IT SELF** but also led to a multitude of fears and these produced chaos, conflict, pain, confusion and as a result - **suffering**.

Suffering, however is the ***blessing*** that insures that the *unconscious* **SELF** <u>**cannot**</u> be eternally **trapped** in the world-dream of separation since suffering eventually turns ITs slumbering consciousness **inward** where IT *remembers* Who IT Really Is.

The dream or sleep that the SELF has experienced is *extremely deep* and has **many layers.** Each one needs to be *exposed and dissolved* in order to move to a deeper Awareness until finally full remembrance of **Who You Really Are** is restored.

When an *Awakening* occurs there is an actual *identity-death-experience* as one *illusion* dissolves and *another* replaces it ... until one is *Truly Free*

These breaking-through experiences are happening for **ALL of humanity** on *some level* during this, **the Great SHIFT** [*the expansion of Conscious Awareness - Awakening*] where what once took eons of clock time to occur is now happening in months and years.

This *little synopsis* briefly summarizes the **three main levels** of that **Awakening.**

CHAPTER ONE

THE CURRENT MASS AWAKENING

Firstly, it is important to know that what is unfolding in each one's experience is **predestined**, sculpted by the *conditioning* that they came in with. Until you arrive at the **second level of Awakening** your predestined experiences *cannot* be changed. Once you are there the *zig-zag pattern* of events becomes like the crow's flight - **straight Home to Freedom.**

When the SELF YOU Are, *descends* into the illusory universe/world and forgets Who IT/YOU is, IT takes on the full weight of the swinging pendulum of **contrast**. This means IT/YOU experiences *every possibility* from **the highest highs to the lowest lows** … IT cannot have one without the other. Some refer to this as **good** and **evil,** however these are **made-up concepts** that attempt to explain the wide swath of **contrasts** that occur within the dream-world based on the belief in separation.

When you ask a question like: *"How can God allow this or that tragedy to happen"* ... this is the reason. Remember, this is YOU *as* God - the ONE SELF experiencing **everything.**

When Consciousness falls into the deepest sleep the **conflict** is *profound* and this manifests in everything from the tiniest family discussion about where to vacation this year or what to have for dinner to global upheavals that involve billions of people. However, since there is **only ONE** the concept of many people is an illusion ... *there are no people, only YOU the ONE SELF seemingly splintered into infinite forms.*

Everything is YOU

Universal Laws

As these myriad of experiences unfold, some *'people'* begin to become aware of how to **manipulate the dream**. They do not know at this stage that it is an *illusion* they are manipulating and so they give this understanding the name **universal laws**.

Since separation engenders the concept of **limitation** [a limited amount of resources to go around], **fear** is *always* present and some of this fear manifests as **selfishness** ... an offshoot of the basic instinct to **survive and propagate.**

In the lowest levels of this instinct many exhibit signs of *ruthlessness, tyranny, and the attempt to totally control* their experiences. Rather than the power this *seems to suggest* to many, it is **extreme weakness** as it reflects the almost *absolute loss of awareness* of the ONE SELF they Are.

There is *no judgment or condemnation* here [*as the body-mind-identity* or **false self** *immediately becomes involved in*], it is simply the way the SELF behaves when it reaches the lowest levels of Conscious Awareness where **extreme imbalance dominates. ALL** have had lifetimes when they lived this way as there is no stone unturned in the expression and experience of life by the SELF in ITs infinite expressions while it sleeps. *This does* **NOT** *mean one should* **agree** **with** *what manifests* **dysfunctionally,** but simply to **NOT** be *attached* to it.

How These Laws Work

When one comes to understand how the dream manifests, whether they are completely *self centered* or have reached a level of *altruism* where they have begun to look out for [so-called] **'others'** ... the same *illusory* laws apply.

Manifestations *within* and *of* the dream happen basically like this:

An idea or concept is desired [some call this a goal]. This is the **INTENTION.**

ATTENTION [focused thought] is applied to this **INTENTION.**

PASSION must be present ... what some call a *Burning Desire.*

BELIEF in this formula must also be present.

When these things are steadily applied to the moldable substance of the universal dream ... manifestation occurs.

Why This Does Not Always Work

What *designs* the **body-mind-identity** or **false self** most refer to as **me** the **person** is a **fabrication** made up out of the

conditioning one has built up over many lifetimes since the original *fall of consciousness.* This conditioning in turn is made up out of one's *[attachments, expectations and identifications tied to memory [the past] and imagination [the future].*

Even if the the so-called universal laws are followed precisely one's conditioning **ALWAYS** colors the *end result* or **INTENTION.** If, for example one's conditioning includes deep feelings of **unworthiness** [the root of ALL conditioning] the **INTENTION** may be realized *and then quickly lost* or it may have sufficient *impetus* to *sabotage* the **INTENTION** altogether.

Nevertheless, many INTENTIONS **do manifest** and as mentioned, are *tainted* by the conditioning of the one or the many that were involved in them.

The Deep State

During the last few hundred years of the *final years* of this era [which is always **dysfunctional** in it decline] ... *the Divine Masculine phase of the Grand Dream,* a group of those who understood how the manifestation process operates and who were deeply asleep to Truth [the SELF They Are], came together to manifest an **INTENTION** called a **One World Order.** Some refer to this group as the **Deep State,** but there are many other names for it.

Over this significant period of clock time the Deep State *infiltrated* and *virtually* **took over** global control of every **key facet** of society that could assist the manifestation of their INTENTION including, *communication [most of the media in all its forms], politics, religion, medicine, drugs [big pharma], fashion, education, agriculture and food production, technology* *including the Internet, entertainment, banking* and much, much more.

Their hold on these industries and services, including many organizations and associations tied to them ... has been **formidable** and has also been a major controlling influence on humanity throughout the entire lifetime of virtually everyone now living on the plant ... mostly in the **unseen.**

At the same time the influence they have wielded, which includes the most insidious aspects of the **patriarchy** [the *dysfunctional* Divine Masculine], that has dominated the planet for thousands of years ... **is rapidly coming to an end** and the planet and humanity are shifting into a *neutral phase* or ***Age of Peace and Light*** *where the Masculine and Feminine influences will be relatively balanced.* This is called **The Great SHIFT** and no matter how it plays out ...

It *IS* Inevitable.

One of the chief components of this **One World Order** is population control and it has been said that a key aspect of the Deep State's INTENTION in that regard is for the planet to ideally have about **500 million people** on it. This requires an enormous *eugenics* project. The aim of eugenics on the surface is to improve the quality of human life but in the end this is simply **massive de-population**.

This entire *PLAN* is now <u>well underway</u>

as this little synopsis is written in 2020

The Plan

Keep in mind again, that there is ***no judgment*** here, the SELF ... *in this case*, is *disguised* as what many would call an **evil**

group and in that respect they would be deemed *to be separate* from the rest of humanity ... but that is **NOT** the case.

Humanity is an illusion as is the entire universe and all this is playing out in **perfect concert** with the **Mass Awakening** now occurring.

There is only ONE [YOU]

appearing as many

As I mentioned earlier, **suffering** is the influence that turns the majority of deep sleepers **inward toward Truth** shifting Awareness from *the head to the Heart* [the SELF]. What is now playing out on the *stage of dreams* are experiences that have significantly *ramped-up* this suffering for most of humanity and it is thereby *battering and shaking* the *deep sleepers*, which is helping to bring about a

What's Really Going On?

Here is **What's Really Going On** *via* this Deep State group of deep sleepers [which is also YOU]:

-enormous *fear* has been spread by the Deep State through the ***introduction of and promotion*** of a **fake pandemic,** which is no more serious than a seasonal flu **[easily verifiable through readily available _real_ statistics provided by world authorities]**

But ... you must do your own research

This **fake pandemic** has spread around the globe causing many areas of the planet to lockdown cities **fostering economic chaos** and promoting **widespread fear,** while expanding **deep psychological challenges.**

Here are some of the

REAL FACTS

related to the fake pandemic

-**99.6%** of people who contracted this **fake pandemic** - **survive** ... making it no more lethal than a **seasonal flu** relative to historical numbers

-*94%* of those who died, **did NOT die** *OF* this **fake pandemic** ... and were only *asymptomatic* [showing no symptoms] **with it**. They died of **preexisting conditions** and were generally 65+ years old

-hospitals were **paid enormous sums** *by the Deep State agencies* to report on death certificates that many *unrelated* deaths were caused by the fake pandemic ... **when they were not**

-the **testing system** used was **NOT** designed for this type of illness and is *often inaccurate*

-80% of those tested were **asymptomatic** ...

The numbers reported have *never* been close to the Truth

-a **highly effective cure** for this illness, with a **100% success ratio** when used in early stages, was **suppressed** by the various arms of the Deep State - especially **medical associations** and the **media**

-**masks** became **mandatory** as a preventative measure despite widespread proof [**also easily verifiable**] that **they do not work.** But they do reduce oxygen, increase CO_2, while **compromising the immune system.** One *globally credible source* reported [based on several months of compiled statistics] that those who wear a mask are **_18 times more likely_** to contract this illness than those who do not

-*masks were also mandatory during the **1918 Spanish flu** that killed **50 million** people. However, most **did NOT die of the Spanish flu,** they died from **bacterial pneumonia _caused by_ wearing masks.** The Deep State knows this*

-all the while **vaccines [*where you have no legal recourse in the event of adverse side effects _as do main stream drugs_]** have been developed that will include an **identifying chip** that can be scanned to prove that you have taken it. **Without that proof** all manner of simple basic needs would be cut off.

-**the media**, almost completely controlled by the Deep State, used continual **spaced repetition** of **mis-information** to further **inflame** the growing fear, panic, paranoia, frustration, anger and depression experienced by the masses

If left to unfold to its end objective [which includes far more sinister aspects], this plan would cause **the total collapse of world economies** leaving only the Deep State's *alternatives* for most of humanity to meekly accept, thereby placing them at the mercy of this **One World Order** plan for **absolute control** ... including its massive **de-population objectives.**

Again ... *this little synopsis is* **NOT** *condemning anyone any more than you would condemn the actors in a dramatic-action-movie you are watching.* **None of this is real.** *That does* **NOT** *mean you should agree with what is playing out any more than you would the so-called bad guys in a movie ...* **it is for you** *to simply recognize it for what it is -* **a dream.**

When the SELF [YOU] descends into the deepest sleep in the dream where IT is **shrouded in many layers of conditioning** and totally forgets *Who IT Really Is,* it is very **easy to manipulate** those who dream at that level.

Deep Sleepers Do Not Resist

Throughout the dream experience of **deep sleepers**, [along with all who linger in the Grand Dream at any level of Conscious Awareness], **ALL** are exposed to **programming** in many, many ways. They are told to believe [often subliminally] what those in power want them to believe. As mentioned, for a few hundred years this powerful group has been *the Deep State* and they have been largely hidden ... **until very recently.**

They have directed **ATTENTION** toward education, food, politics, entertainment, health, finance and behaviour on a multitude of subjects that eventually dovetails into their specific agenda, oriented in some way to the control and manipulation of the masses. **Advertising , entertainment and the media are prime instruments** to accomplish these objectives through *spaced repetition* of their manipulating concepts. Repetition has always been a powerful method [in the dream] *for sculpting behavior.*

Heavily promoted concepts [such as masks and social distancing] become *trends,* which ultimately are *accepted as **normal** social behaviors.*

Once a behavior is **accepted** [often in as little as a few months] it is difficult to persuade a deep sleeper that it is **NOT** in their best interests to continue with that practice. The behavior has, by then been hard-wired *into their conditioning* and becomes part of *who they believe they* *are* ... even to the point of them aggressively *defending* it.

Complete **denial** is also an aspect of the **heaviest** of deep sleepers ... the total absence of **a need or desire to know** anything different than **the current narrative.** Such is the **abject fear** of many deep sleepers who are terrified of having even the most uncomfortable but **familiar circumstances** disturbed. Its a scenario of *the enemy you know rather than one you do not know - the UNKNOWN.*

This can easily be recognized in the more advanced versions of programming called **addiction** where even if the deep sleeper knows that something is derogatory for their well-being they continue to pursue it.

When behavior reaches addiction [not just drugs for example but with simple everyday things like cell phone usage and junk food], there is **little or no resistance** and all manner of solutions are then offered that *in many cases* take the deep sleeper even further under the thumb of those in control. *This is a concept of* **manifesting problems** *that are* **not real** *and then* **providing solutions** *for them that ties one even tighter to the perpetrator.*

This is precisely what occurred with this Deep State man-made illness

The current fake pandemic is **a blatant example** of this highly effective procedure on a global scale.

REMEMBER

... all the players on the stage are

YOU [SELF]

Unknown to the deep sleeping Deep State, this nefarious global **plan** *is also offering the* *catalyst,* which is providing the **necessary degree of _suffering_** [the profound and constant **SHAKING of circumstances**] *to take the* **mass of deep sleepers** *to the* **line in the sand** *where a*

BREAKTHROUGH is possible.

The SHIFT Is Near

Right now that *line in the sand* is very near. There is a **global push-back** by many high profile sources who have **much to lose** but have arrived at the point where they cannot so-called *live with themselves* **if they do no speak out.**

This includes in particular, thousands of **doctors** around the world combined with **politicians, reporters and lawyers** who are *risking their reputations, credentials* and *careers* to speak out about **the Real facts.**

This is the ***first sign*** of what later is an ***essential*** aspect of the **second level of Awareness [Awakening]** that ultimately becomes **Freedom** [remembering Who You Really Are] ...

Absolute

Transparency **and** *Authenticity*

NO MATTER WHAT

Critical Point

What is about to occur is a **MASS AWAKENING** to what the *world's deep sleepers believed was reality all their lives* ... **IS NOT.**

Whether this unfolds in a **highly protracted** and **inflamed** manner or in a somewhat more **subdued and benign** way is not the point. A **critical-point** juncture for **MASS**

AWAKENING *is very near* and will bring billions of deep sleepers [the bulk of humanity (yet still ONE)] to a major **SHIFT of Awareness** that the world they have known is far different than they believed it was.

For *most,* this will ultimately be a **SHIFT** that is *Joyous* as the world moves into an **Age of Light** bringing with it *balance* that has not been known for thousands of years. For them it will be like a *dream coming true, nevertheless* **still** *a dream* ... and they will continue on sleeping in a **different dream.**

For some however, this Awareness **[Awakening]** will be *very* **unsettling** and cause *considerable* **disorientation**. During this **SHIFT** the mind [the false self, with all its conditioning], is being and will be **shaken even more severely**. This can feel like one is **going crazy** [losing their mind] and that is precisely what is required for one to be

OPEN and available for Truth to enter ... *the mind has to be lost,* meaning lost to it role *as* your identity ...

so that one then thinks/feels

through the Heart [SELF]

For these ones, this will be the precursor to the **Second level of Awakening.**

CHAPTER TWO

THE SECOND AWAKENING

A relatively *small percentage* of humanity has already awoken from the **deep sleep** that the world they live in is **NOT** *what they believed* it was and they are being pulled by the same *end-of-an-era* **SHIFT** into the **Second Awakening**. Those few who are **sufficiently shaken** by the **first Awakening** will join this group.

This group have for years in many cases, [as this rapidly expanding **age of Peace and Light** has been unfolding], *sensed* that **this world is a dream.** The **mind [false self]** however, has spent many dream-lifetimes immersed in the Grand Dream and this concept is, at this point, ***only a mental concept.*** As a result, they are *'dancing at two weddings'* ... with one foot in the **Grand**

Dream and the other headed toward **Reality.**

Lip-service is therefore paid to this **new concept** as each one enters and/or participates in what may be referred to as - a *spiritual life.* In most cases this usually occurs **outside** of organized religion with its dogma that is often slanted, confined and even highly judgmental.

This new spiritual focus becomes an *adjunct* to the day-to-day life experience of so-called **surviving and hopefully thriving** that they, as the **body-mind-identity [person]** <u>**still believes**</u> is who they are. In this respect, spirituality becomes a benign way *to make their dream-life* **more comfortable and cozy.**

These *'people'* [remember, there **are** no people ... only ONE/YOU appearing as many], usually find themselves devouring a multitude of ancient and/or recent teachings surrounding spiritual concepts, which include many, many disciplines like yoga, breathing techniques, strict food regimes, meditation, healing concepts that are naturally oriented, daily disciplines and practices, mantras, chanting and a host of concepts often led by so-called *'advanced'* teachers called gurus.

In *most cases* the belief systems at this level of Awareness place the remembrance of **Who YOU Really Are** <u>*out in the future*</u> *where is does* **NOT** *exist* ... and dream-lifetimes are spent pursuing these concepts.

Many of the *'people'* who are spiritually oriented at this *level of Awareness* **[Awakening]** become what are called **spiritual activists** where many spiritual methods are attempted to try to **fix the world** and **save** other *'people'*. They are not yet Aware that the **conditioning** that manifests **the world** and the **behavior** of every dreamer ___must___ be **dissolved** before **Real change occurs.**

Conditioning that is NOT dissolved

___always___ finds another way to manifest

Nevertheless, **IF** there is a feeling of **Joy** associated with these activities then, *for the moment* ... that is where one belongs. The **Presence of Joy** is always the **indicator** that *validates* that one is *in-the-flow* of **their destiny.** *[Joy is not the same thing as happiness, which always dances with sorrow on a roller coaster of ups and downs].*

Many at this level of Awareness very soon begin to *'teach'*, having acquired what the false self believes are **special abilities**. This subtly *fosters the belief* in **separation**, which is the **primary cause** behind the manifestation of the Grand Dream. In their *well-meaning* attempt to help *'others' while they too are still conditioned and dreaming,* they place new **links** in the **chains** that bind them to the dream-world.

Again, if the **Joy** factor is present then this **is** part of their *predestined life experience.*

Many *dream-lifetimes* are often spent in this way until finally a level of ***satiation*** *is reached* that brings them to **a breakthrough.** It is at this point that the **fear of Surrender** to the **Unknown** and what may lie beyond *is* <u>*less than*</u> the **deep frustration and misery** of a life that has **NOT** brought them to <u>**unbroken**</u> **Joy, Peace, Love and Freedom** *that they may have* had **many vignettes** of ...

But which did not last.

They may waffle back and forth for many more years before making the **NO MATTER WHAT** choice to be **Free** [*fully Awakened to Who They Really Are*] ... such is the ***abject fear*** associated with this choice. The reason is because this choice leads to **death** ... not of the body but of **the identity** and it is the fear of being **'*nothing*'** or *ceasing to exist that is the greater fear.*

Millions, still relatively few in proportion to the global population [nevertheless, still ONE], *are now approaching this choice that will bring them to the **Second Awakening*** as the enormous influence of **the Great SHIFT** now taking place ***expands rapidly***.

When this choice is made **humbly and sincerely,** the **mental belief** that the world/universe is a dream soon becomes a **Heart-centered Knowing**. From then on, there is ***no turning back.***

Belief, Faith and Trust

still engender some doubt

but KNOWING has no doubt whatsoever

and burns ALL bridges

CHAPTER THREE

THE 'REAL' AWAKENING - FREEDOM

When the **AHA moment** arrives where you **KNOW** that the *universe/world* is a dream ... *you are* **FREE** and this is the **second Awakening.** There is *no supposition or theory* about this ... it is the **total Awareness [Awakening]** that it is an **illusion** through the **Heart [the SELF].**

Imagine the world you have experienced as a **theater** in which you as the **body-mind-identity** *you have believed was who you are* as a **person [the false self],** acted out your day to day dream life *totally believing* it was real. *This is currently the Awareness level most of humanity.*

When you **KNOW** the universe/world is a dream [not just as a mental concept you believe in], *you step **off the stage** as the player* ... **asleep in the dream** and become **semi-conscious - Free** but still with the **baggage of conditioning** that *manifested* this **false self** and your **unique** dream. You are now **witnessing** the dream **tethered** only by your **conditioning** to it.

Remember, ***conditioning*** *is made up of attachments, expectations and identifications tied to memory [the past] and imagination [the future].* These are the chains that bind you to the dream and which *bring you,* as the **slumbering God-SELF** *back* again and again into dream bodies in the **Grand Dream**.

Most refer to **conditioning** as **karma** but this word has many *confusing connotations* and this little synopsis is meant to be absolutely **simple** and **clear,** and so the word **conditioning** is used.

Returning to **another body** in the Grand Dream is referred to as **reincarnation** and yet it too *is a dream* since nothing **REAL** has a beginning and an ending. Nevertheless, <u>*within*</u> the dream ... it is real **as** a dream.

At this **second** stage of **Awareness [Awakening]** the *line in the sand* has usually been crossed that says: **"I choose Freedom NO MATTER WHAT"**. If it **has not** been crossed it soon will be with this **KNOWING.**

The **ATTENTION** that has been placed on the **dream** and **colored by the conditioning baggage** you came in with and have added to since you arrived in this particular body, now shifts to

totally **dissolving this conditioning.**

If you think of this *conditioning baggage* as **clouds** that are **hiding the ever-Present sun [the SELF You Are]** that when dissolved, simply **reveal** what has *always been there,* then you will *become aware* that when this occurs the **Real YOU** *will be exposed* ... **YOU** will **Realize** that **IT is YOU** ...

the God You Are or ONE SELF

That Awareness is the **third** or **REAL AWAKENING**, which is also known as **Self Realization.**

Journey Without Distance

This **conscious** pathless-path starts with whatever **conditioning baggage** you had when you stepped off the stage of dreams and as *layer after of layer* of this *conditioning* is dissolved you metaphorically move further up into the theater with only **echoes** of *conditioning* remaining.

At this level of Awareness very little that occurs in the dream *molests* the **Peace [SELF] You Are.** You see clearly that the dream-world you thought real for so long **IS** an *illusion* and you are **triggered** *far more often* by your remaining conditioning since you have become

very sensitive to

who you are NOT

As a result you move very soon to the *upper balcony* of the theater and receive only occasional **whispers** of **conditioning** like a dream-aroma wafting past your inner senses.

The **SHIFT** that is now *rapidly occurring*, is heavily **_SHAKING_** every corner of the world-dream, and is therefore powerfully **pulling humanity** into one of the three **Awakening** levels depending on which one you **[the slumbering God-SELF]** are currently approaching.

Shifting from one level of **Awareness [Awakening]** to another seems like an *evolution* or a *becoming* **[which suggests time and space, which engenders separation]** ... but it is **NOT.**

ONE is always ONE and has *no divisions* of any kind. It is the **mind [false self]** that sees *division* or *separation* and therefore intervals of *time and space* to get from where it seems to be to somewhere else. Again, this is an illusory aspect of **dreaming.**

YOU as ONE _go_ no where

Dissolving Conditioning

As mentioned in Chapter Two, there are a multitude of **spiritual concepts, systems and disciplines** available and practiced by millions around the globe to either *make their dream world more comfortable* in a benign way or to *attempt to arrive at* this **Self Realization Awareness [Awakening].**

However, unless a system acknowledges that Freedom is **ever-Present Now**, it will **NEVER** lead one **Home** to the **Freedom** of the **ONE SELF.**

"Other than **Self Inquiry,** *there are* **no adequate means** *to make the mind [false self]* **permanently subside.**" – Ramana

Many exquisitely beautiful spiritual systems and practices exist that **WILL** bring about **temporary vignettes** of this **Awareness** and many aspirants *have experienced* this ... and perhaps often ... but, *when the practice ends* ultimately they return to the level of Awareness they had before.

Nevertheless, many practices such as **meditation** *do have* the benefit of bringing about **One-Pointedness** and this *does* make **Self Inquiry/Surrender** much simpler.

Self Inquiry Explained Simply

Here is the **simplicity** of the **Self Inquiry** practice. Because it is so simple, *many cannot comprehend* that it is so **powerful** and **effective** in **dissolving** the many layers of conditioning that make up the false self dream.

Thought

When **any thought** _triggers_ you and gets your **attention** you simply ask, **"To whom does this thought arise?"**

The Answer

The obvious and **only** answer is always:

_"Me."_

Question

This is followed by the question, **"Who am I?"** However, _no attempt_ **to answer** this question _is ever made._

What is occurring is this ... the false-self-identity has been _hiding in plain sight_ for eons because almost everyone believes _it is_ who they are and have never questioned this.

When the false self is **continually exposed** in this way it **withdraws back into the SELF** from where it arose and eventually **dissolves** altogether ... **revealing the ONE SELF** as **Who You Really Are.**

Surrender Explained Simply

When **absolute Surrender** [*allowing Life [the SELF] to Live Life*] is added to **Self Inquiry** ... the pathless-path Home is very rapid. Vigilance is required but Freedom is very near. In and of itself, **Surrender** is also a pathless-path Home and WILL lead one to the *Freedom* **They Are Now** as well. **Self Inquiry and Surrender** are like two sides of the same coin.

Surrender is simply allowing the **SELF** or **Life** or **God** or **ONE** [whatever name works for you] to totally *run the show* ... _no exceptions._ You hold onto *no decision* *making* of any kind and defer to the **Still Small Voice of Silence [the SELF]** *to orchestrate* every breath. This was the route I chose.

This is your **ONLY Purpose** for being here *until it is achieved*. Every other so-called purpose is *an illusion* and a *distraction* from this one Purpose ... total **Awakening** to **Who You Really Are - the ONE SELF.**

Full Awareness of the SELF - ONE

... YOU Are,

is the third Awakening

ABOUT THE AUTHOR

John McIntosh

As an entrepreneur multi-millionaire until 1999 John traveled for decades around the world speaking to tens of thousands of people about Personal Development before *leaving everything* behind and *surrendering totally* to the SELF.

John shares his acquired understanding of the false self identity together with his personal experience of thinking with the Heart, which returns you to full Conscious Awareness of Who You Really Are through his 29 books and daily Blog articles as well regular Online Q&A discussions.

LINKS

BOOKS by John McIntosh

https://www.johnmcintosh.info/copy-of-books

SUBSCRIBE to John McIntosh's daily BLOG

https://www.johnmcintosh.info/subscribe

Q@A ONLINE VIDEO Re-Plays

https://www.one-self.info/q-a-online

TESTIMONIALS

I've been reading spiritual books for decades. I've read most of the best authors, but none has been as clear as John's books.
- Rod Spain

John writes from his Heart with such incredible inspirational power. - Wendy Embleton Huber

You are as clear and direct a teacher as I've come across - Alex Alioto

Amazing writing. I feel it in my Heart. - Irina Isakov

Such clarity and simplicity in your ability to communicate the Truth. Christine Van Hoose